A play by Julia Donaldson
Illustrated by Igor Sinkovec

Patient 1: Doctor, doctor! I've broken my arm in two places.

Doctor: Well, don't go back **there** again.

Nurse: Next, please!

Patient 4: Doctor, doctor! My son has swallowed my pen. What should I do?

Doctor: Try using a pencil.

Nurse: Next, please!

Patient 3: Doctor, doctor! I swallowed a bone.

Doctor: Are you choking?

Patient 3: No, I really did!

Nurse: Next, please!

Patient 2: Doctor, doctor! I can't get to sleep.

Doctor: Try sitting on the edge of the bed and you'll soon drop off.

Nurse: Next, please!

Patient 1: Doctor, doctor! I feel like a bell.

Doctor: Take these pills, and if they don't help, give me a ring!

Nurse: Next, please!

Patient 4: Doctor, doctor! I feel like a pair of curtains.

Doctor: Pull yourself together!

Nurse: Next, please!

Patient 1: Doctor, doctor! I snore so loudly I keep myself awake.

Doctor: Try sleeping in another room then.

Nurse: Next, please!

Patient 2: Doctor, doctor! I keep thinking there are two of me.

Doctor: Don't both speak at once!

Nurse: Next, please!

Patient 3: Doctor, doctor! I keep thinking I'm invisible.

Doctor: Who said that?

Nurse: Next, please!

Patient 4: Doctor, doctor! I've lost my memory!

Doctor: When did this happen?

Patient 4: When did what happen?

Nurse: Next, please!

Patient 2: Doctor, doctor! I feel like a vampire.

Nurse: Necks, please!

Patient 3: Doctor, doctor! I keep thinking I'm a dog.

Nurse: Sit!

Doctor: How long have you felt like this?

Patient 3: Ever since I was a puppy.

Patient 1: Doctor, doctor! How do I stop my nose from running?

Doctor: Stick your foot out and trip it up!

Nurse: Next, please!

12

Patient 3: Doctor, doctor! My sister thinks she's a lift!

Doctor: Well, ask her to come in, then.

Patient 3: I can't – she doesn't stop at this floor!

Nurse: Next, please!

Patient 4: Doctor, doctor! I keep getting a pain in my eye when I drink coffee!

Doctor: Have you tried taking the spoon out of the cup first?

Nurse: Next, please!

Patient 2: Doctor, doctor! I think I'm a bridge.

Doctor: What's come over you?

Patient 2: Oh, two cars, a large truck and a coach.

Nurse: Next, please!

Patient 1: Doctor, doctor! I keep thinking I'm a pack of cards.

Doctor: I'll deal with you later.

Nurse: Next, please!

Patient 2: Doctor, doctor! I've run out of hankies. What can I use?

Nurse: A-tishoo!

Patient 1: Doctor, doctor! I keep seeing this insect flying round and round my head.

Doctor: Don't worry, it's just a bug that's going round.

Nurse: A-tishoo! Doctor, doctor! I think I've caught something.

Doctor: Well, if it's only a little one you'd better throw it back in the water.

Nurse: Next, please!

Doctor: No, wait! I can't take much more of this. Are there still a lot of patients in the waiting room?

Nurse: Well, there are quite a lot who think they are bees.

Doctor: Oh no! How many?

Nurse: A whole swarm.

Doctor: Can you get rid of them?

Nurse: I'll try. Buzz off, you lot!

Doctor: Thank you.

Nurse: Next, please!

Patient 2: Doctor, doctor! I feel terrible. You've got to help me out.

Doctor: Certainly. Here's the door – and I think I'll go with you. I've had enough for one day!

Nurse: Me too!

They all exit.